A Life Of Poetry

Angie Parker

Dedication

To my Mom, my sisters and the ones who never stopped inspiring me to write

9-11

So many dreams become a cloud of dust
A loss of life, a loss of trust
The question, where do we go from here
So many pieces, so many tears

All the years lost in this day
Pulling together to find a way
A sigh of despair, the skies are pale
The night's empty, as the buildings fell

A tear falls from a child's eyes
The dreams we gave her, were they lies
A father gone, a mother mourns
We grieve together, a nation torn

A proud country, as we unite
Rebuild the dreams, and fight the fight
Heroes rise from the dust and dark
Through our pain, there is a spark

To stand together, strong and tall
Against the terror that changed us all
To honor the ones who were so brave
To fight for them and the world they saved.

Special Ones

There are certain people
who simply come and go
but they leave behind a memory
that you never could let go
And then there are some people
who brought a smile along the way
who made the most of everything
and brightened up your day
And then there are those moments
when you wonder where they've gone
but know you'll always hold them
and that the spirit will live on
For sometimes they come and go so quick
we simply don't realize what they meant
but forever there will be a place
where their tenderness is sent
And when we finally realize
that each step in life is ours
then in each moment when we meet the one
who was once our shining star
We would place them in a special place
and always keep them near
And when they had to go away
we would hold their message here
So when you find someone who holds you
and comforts you through the night
and brings to you a smile
that makes everything all right
Then don't forget to place them
where the heart holds them secure
remember them in their purest form
for in sorrow they were the cure...

Threads

Silver moon shine in my soul
Replace the dream that someone stole
Golden sun shade my heart
From those thieves who've torn me apart.

Dim sweet starlight come to me
take my wish, show me the key
Bluest waters, share your tide
rushing waves, don't let me hide.

Burning sand, so white and pure
hot to touch, beauty your lure.
Songbird sing sweet melodies
Take me back, oh won't you please.

Inhibitions

There is something warm inside of me
when the alcohol goes down
there is something so alive in me
when I go out on the town
somehow there's no fear inside
and I just feel so free
I say the things I long to say
that are locked deep inside of me
and sometimes I regret things
because I feel so naive
but I tell you how I really feel
and then you turn and leave
And then I start to thinking
that you just don't really care
You just don't pay attention
to the things I try to share
And I sit and wonder why I stay
or why on earth I'm there
for only in my dreams at night
could you take me anywhere
And you always seem to avoid me
and I just close my eyes
so I can't see the truth in you
I keep telling myself lies
But the truth is you don't love me
and you don't want me near
I guess you tried to show it
and the message is quite clear
but I keep hoping for a sign somewhere
that says one day you'll see
there really is a special place
deep inside of me.

Stranger's Words

So many feelings rushing through me
and the reason is yet to be told
Only know the words you've written
are the dreams to which I hold.
My laughter is the answer
to the question in my heart
That subtle shine inside my soul
says something's about to start.
It isn't just the words, you see
it's all the little things
It's the way you shine inside of me
and the inspiration that you bring.
Alone at night I often think
of one day being there
To meet the man who touches me
with the many thoughts you've shared
I do not think, whether right or wrong
though you have a place in my heart's deep well
And the passion in the words I say
I trust in time, eternity shall tell
Though so far away, you seem to be
I always feel somehow you're near
And I hope you know this love I feel
and one day it brings you here
Though, only a short time has gone
since that first time we met
You see, I feel a little weak inside
this may be the only chance I get.
And so I've chosen to tell you now
and hope in some way you feel it too
Though, I've fallen for the dreams and words
those words, they came from you.
And when I think about that thought
and how my emotions want to abide
I see no reason to leave my love unspoken
for I have no fear that I should hide.

Thread of Life

Clouds of doubt creep inside my head
Nothing to hold me but one silver thread
Not gold, nor shiny, it's not the best
But it held on, and it outlived the rest
To be the wall and keep me safe
to fight the thieves and leave no trace
The one never spoken, a hurtful word
the one who helped beggars, who listened and heard
The thin silver lining that's part of my soul
the thread of life, it keeps me whole.

Promise Me

Promise me forever
and I promise no regrets
Promise me a rainbow
and I promise I won't forget.
Believe in me always
and I will give, to you, my heart
Believe in making memories
and we will never be apart.
Dream of silent moments
when the words are in our souls
Dream of such sweet passion
for together we are whole.
Whisper to me softly
all the hopes you want to share
Whisper through the darkness
because you know I will be there.
Kiss me slow and gently
and let your warmth draw me near
Kiss away my sorrows
and I will take away your fear.
Hold me closely in your arms
and be with me tonight
Hold my heart inside of you
and I'll not question if it's right
Be patient in your waiting
for I am patiently awaiting too
And patience let's this feeling grow
and reveals my love for you.

Heartfelt Fight

Wonder why it happens
that we can't help the things we
said
Wonder why our frustration
makes us hurt others instead
Can we not see them crying
or is it just nice that they hurt
too
I'd rather write them in a book
then have my problems upset
you
You make me feel so empty
and you make me feel so small
Like I could not be good
enough
am I no good at all?
I never heard you tell me
that you like who I am
Only remember all the words
when you said you didn't give a
damn
Wonder why you'd even say it
if you didn't think it true
Anyway, now you have hurt me
is that what you meant to do?
Yes you have left me crying

and now you have walked out of
the door
I guess you've said it all now
and you don't want to look at
me anymore
Well I hope that you feel better
and your anger is no longer
inside
Because you've passed it on to
me
and I've gone away to hide
It doesn't make me feel good
when there are other places I
could be
**But I am sure next time you're
angry**
you will come and look for me
**And I guess that I should take
it**
since you have made it all so
clear
I am all of nothing, so...
I'll still be standing here.
I have to lay down here now
and make myself believe
that I am still somebody too
and one day, I will just leave.

Little Girl Lost

Deep inside this heart she hides
and chases her chance away
Didn't know she was passing by
her dream for better days.

Somehow she'd lost the little girl
who played and loved and laughed
Forgotten how to smile at life
because her life was ripped in half.

Now she struggles through every hour
trying to know her path
Always skeptical of the roads to choose
for will they lead to someone's wrath

Hiding in the darkest corners
disguised by a mysterious mask
Running from the obvious questions
she fears someone will ask.

Never looking into the mirror
too afraid of what's in the glass
if she is passive through the days
she hopes her time will pass.

But one day she knows, is coming
when her fears come face to face
And there's no closing her eyes now
she must go back to that place

Maybe she won't find her answers
but she may just find herself
And grow to dream the dreams she keeps
high upon that dusty shelf.

Gothic Lover

Flash of touch, the searing flames
Lost in darkness...forgotten names
Drink the warmth, sucking blood
Washed in sin, a passionate flood.

Sharp as teeth to bite thy neck
Eat the flesh, a bloody wreck
Deep, purple black night of lust
Tomorrow memories of tonight are dust

Stolen kisses, he walks the night
Mysteries of death, art, fear takes flight
Urging to swallow all that he is
Knowing in his world, my unknowing lives

Wanting his breath, steal mine away
consume eachother more every day
His blackness intriguing, wanting it, mine
Sway him to touch me with black velvet and wine

Lips of sweet venom, eyes of coal
Vampire tempting...take me into the black hole
Passion, pain, mystery...such immense desire
he takes my soul, flesh consumed in fire.

Made to See

With just a glance
she feels his fire
unknown inside her
such sin and desire
Consume him, taste him
bring him inside
Her fear for loving
and passions abide
Allow her to feel
his moment of pain
But to feel good is torture
he knows not her name
Using the sin
to forget the burden within
it's wrong to feel good
when the darkness begins
Spinning her web
of self hate and lies
He makes her see him
makes her open her eyes.

The Real Me

All that I am is jaded
not really me at all
All that is me is hidden
about to take the fall
If I don't open up my eyes
and live my life
Everything will become painful
and I hold the knife
Sometimes it makes me feel good
but it's just sex
No one is holding me in the morning
what do I expect?
They never saw something special
they looked through me
Nothing beautiful or amazing
nothing is what they see
Ah, yes the art of making love
but with no emotion
Pleasure, passion...they give it all
with no devotion
I thought something would make me feel good
not this way
I wanted to believe in me again
what can I say?
A whore is what I've made myself
I must turn my face
Nothing pleasant about my thinking
I must leave this place
Burn the dreams of being loved
or held in the night
Forget the wishful thoughts of life
without the bitter fight.
9-11-99

"You with the sad eyes, don't be discouraged...oh I realize it's hard to take courage. In a world full of people you can lose sight of it all, the darkness inside you can make you feel so small...but I see your true colors shining through...I see your true colors and that's why I love you...so don't be afraid to let them show...Your true colors...true colors...are beautiful like a rainbow"
Cindy Lauper

World in You

I see waterfalls of green and blue
I see the truth, when I look at you
Beautiful and gentle, patient and smart
Piercing my soul, reading my heart

Color of rainbows, sparkling and pure
Crystals of sunshine, that heal and cure
Showing emotions you long to hide
Showing the world, being your guide

Capturing moments, to save in your mind
looking inside me, my thoughts left behind
Holding the answers, keeping no lies
I see all of this when I look in your eyes.

I Never Knew

I never knew what I had lost
until I felt this way for you
I didn't think I was missing much
or what wonderful things the heart could do

I just made believe I was ok
to never feel such love again
But now to feel so high and free
I feel I have a new place to begin

And I'm not afraid to try this
and to share so much of me
For broken, kept or just ignored
to feel again, is all it could be

And I feel for you such great things
that I can't begin to say
for words could do no justice here
and silence has a way.

My Last Year

If in this life, I cease to live
and through my tears I cease to give
Then there would be nothing left of me
that's good and real for my friends to see

If in this time, my world stands still
and I let my pain make me cease to feel
Then I am not living, I no longer care
if the dreams inside, I cannot share.

If in this day, I have no golden light
then my warmth won't comfort my friends tonight
if my arms don't long to hold him near
then I have died and turned from my fear.

If in this world, I cannot smile
and help someone to laugh for just awhile
If I cannot look clearly into his eyes
then I have given way to all the lies

If in this life I find no peace
and through experience, my pains don't cease
then I shall close my eyes without a tear
and say farewell to this, my last year.

Secret Path

I have a secret path I take
no one knows about but me
I go there sometimes to clear my mind
and to set old memories free

A pathway filled with wildflowers
where their sweetness has a chance
Where I am free to look inside
and alone to learn life's dance

A garden grown of honesty
and blossoming in trust
Brought about by dreams and wishes
that once started out as dust.

Solitude is such splendor
and the hope becomes a flame
Making my soul so wild and free
there's no place quite the same

To walk along the stony path
alone in quiet peace
and fill my spirit with such clarity
that all bad things shall cease

This is my secret pathway
where all my dreams shall be
and patience waits my sweet return
to this place I've made for me.

5/99

For Sadness Asks Why

A sudden sense of lonely
hides behind these eyes
A world has left me trembling
no answers to my why's

A single candle holds me
from the rage I feel inside
A memory I'm afraid of
untouched and left behind.

A web of my confusion
when I had just begun to trust
All my fears revisited
and hopes have turned to dust

Each night so dark and chilling
and days just pass me by
Embraced by such sadness
as I sit alone and cry

For all the purest faces
flashing across the screen
And not one could give me comfort
for the pain I have just seen

Turmoil in this tragedy
and hurt they've never known
I only hope to reach out to them
so they know they're not alone.

tribute to Columbine High School

Scared To Love You

Sometimes I get so nervous
that I just run and hide
Sometimes I'm scared of feeling
all this love I feel inside
Sometimes I can remember
what feeling so good, often brought
Sometimes it brought tears to me
for love brings pain, a lot.
Sometimes the words are held
tightly within my soul
Sometimes I think you have brought
back the words someone once stole
And sometimes I can be quiet
for my silence says it well
Sometimes the things I leave unspoken
have a story still to tell.
For sometimes love is lost in time
or has crept away somewhere
But if you just give me the chance
you'll find the words are there.

For Sean...12/10/99

Would It Be Too Much

Would it be too much to ask
If I could be with you
Would I be out of line if I
wanted to give something to you?

Would it be too awkward
if I wanted to share
Would it be inappropriate
to tell you that I care?

Would it be too big a deal if I
wanted to hold you close
Would I be called crazy if..
I said you meant the most?

12/10/99

Lost

Could the rain wash out the sorrow
that I feel through every day?
Could the sun's light dry the tears I cry
and help me find my way?

Might there be an answer
to the questions in my heart
Might I, one day, hear the laughter
that could help my life to start?

Should the world spin all around me
and leave me silent and alone
Should my dreams die inside of me
because I am on my own?

Would the grass seem greener
if I showered it with love
Would my taste of life be sweeter
if I had helped from up above?

Could the rain drown out the sorrow
that I feel so strong today
Could the sunlight dry my teary eyes
and let me know my way?

9/22/97

Coma

One night I closed my eyes to sleep
and something held them tight
A thousand dreams of nothing came
and tried to steal my light.

Their tears fell free around me
and still nothing rose within
Their faces filled of love and fear
that I might not let them in.

Though my spirit tried to reach you
something held my voice
I never meant to frighten you
but the night gave me no choice.

All my pleading words, unspoken
and the truth was left untold
My life fell to the hands of fate
and your love I had to hold.

I tried to say "I love you",
and tried to tell you not to go
Did I somehow make you feel it
or did you never know?

I wanted to come back to you
I left so many things behind
But if God had planned it different
then still I keep you in my mind.

8/97

Spiral

Falling
faster, faster faster
Plummeting
into this unknown world.
Darkness
settling into the soul
Rotted flesh, smoldering
the smell of death...
so
near.
Crawling, groveling, clinging
Hands
holding to a thread
Golden thread of life
Sinking
beneath the frozen foot
is the swampy
ground.

Silent Eyes

I always look behind me
for I feel someone is there
I feel his eyes all over me
but I can't see him anywhere.

I can smell his anger
locked so deep inside his soul
He had to feel the power
and so, my life, he stole.

I can taste the warmth and sweetness
of the blood he took from me
But the scars upon my spirit
are the wounds I can't set free.

I still feel the stinging touch
of all those pleading tears
and death lay gently beside me
and brought to me, this lasting fear.

For now, I feel I'm nothing
my shattered pieces on the floor
Once I knew a trusted world
now I have nothing to live for.

Darkness feels so evil now
and still I am searching for the light
And throughout life's misery
one day I will win this fight.

1997

Don't Blame Me

What was I wearing, did I lead him on?
What was I thinking to drive him around so long?
Did I try and fight him, or did I give in?
If I had fought harder, did you think I might win?

Why couldn't I run and why couldn't I scream?
You think I exaggerate and go to extremes.
STOP!!! Stop and listen, do you hear what you say?
Do not tell me you know, what I went through that day.

Did you feel the sting of his fists hit my face?
Did you feel the chill of the night and that place?
Did you feel my fear, as I felt the death?
As he lay over me, could you smell his soured breath?

You could not have felt this...and it's just too late for advice
For that night lost my innocence, and I pay that price.

1996

Somewhere

Sometimes this world gets lonely
something cries out from within
somewhere between here and there
when might my life begin?
Just going through the motions
I try and find my way
Fighting through another hour
just to live another day.
Another night in silence
inside my burning dreams
Is this world so tedious
is life all that it seems?
I saw the lights of Vegas
as they slowly filled my soul
Now in the quiet starlight
I do not feel quite whole
My heart holds an empty space
that I fill with work all day
Somehow, someday I'll be there
and that is where I'll stay.

1997

Nature Grows

(A child's mind wrote this)

Nature lives and nature grows
with flowers bunched in many rows
With corn as sweet as sugarcanes
and horses with their beautiful manes.

Nature is a masterpiece
say my uncle and my niece
With birds singing in the trees
and lions out running free

Nature lives and nature grows
like flowers bunched in many rows
where life is beautiful, as it seems
and we can all live out our wildest dreams.

Blindness

I could see it all so clearly
but I chose to close my eyes
As you mused upon your jealousy
something about you died
Each word you left unspoken
played like a record on my mind
every call you contemplated
was there for me to find.
The little hints of anger
and sarcasm in your tone
They made my awareness stronger
that you feared to be alone.
Each time the game was played
you compelled yourself to cheat
For winning was the only way
but now you face defeat.

1998

A Thought

Try to understand me
do you think you can?
Stop playing like a little boy
stand up and be a man

Must you take a drink this time
are you strong enough?
Forget about the consequence
maybe you're not so tough.

Spirit Past

There is a spirit locked inside of me
crying out to be free
To my beating heart, it sends this message
and hopes that I will see
I feel the light of burning dreams
trying so hard to live
Inside this crazy world, I wonder
is it only what you give?
Trying to hold on to the memories
the ones that made me smile
when my heart starts losing sight again
I can dream for just awhile

Whisper of Emotion

What are you dreaming with your eyes closed so tight?
Of who are you thinking, am I on your mind tonight?
Your laughter, so contagious, it takes my breath away
All that I can think is how I hope that you will stay.
I do not think you know me, or what I need to say
With you I feel a lifetime in every single day
Your eyes hide so well just how you feel inside
I remember when I met you, it was the first day in my life.

A Cure

There are times I am uncertain
about life's little mysteries
Why must our people hunger
and why are some diseased

A plague of death settles in our lives
why do we not think twice
As love once warmed our hearts
and now it's cold as ice.

There are many painful moments
that we are to endure
why accept a world that's dying
instead of searching for the cure?

Could we really be forgetting
are we truly giving in?
Take the time to look within you
and help to find an end.

1992

Just Imagine

When I feel a little lonely
as if nothing will ever be quite right
I just close my eyes and imagine
Heaven's angels and God's great light

For I am certain each time I falter
and every thought of doubt I feel
There is a hand outstretched, to calm me
comfort and peace I know is real

Sometimes when darkness frightens me
and that strange knot grips me inside
I hear a soft, reassuring voice
and believe again, this is my guide

Each morning as I feel the sun's warmth
It is the smile to start my day
It brings the lost hope back to my life
and wills me to know the way.

Confusion

Round and round
the world
does spin
Life goes down
we cannot win
Up and up
the balloon
shall fly
Lost in time
we say good bye
Side to side
the wind
shall blow
Never knowing
which way we'll
go.

This Moment

If there ever was a moment when I needed to feel your hand
it must be this moment when your presence would help me stand
If I ever felt so empty, it must be this day
When you turned your love from me, and in a moment slipped away
If there was a night of silence, when a heart was forced to break
Tonight you scar my innocence, it is my heart that you forsake
If ever there was a place in time, when all bad things could be erased
I would clear away the foolish thoughts, I thought you could replace
If you ever really needed me, in this moment ... I am here
And in the second that you turn from me, I have disappeared.

Father

Through these eyes of dusted dreams
came pictures of a time
Purple clouds that crept within
and broke up the dirt and grime
A crystal blue came through the haze
like a ray of mystic light
Reality reaches out to my view
innocent eyes, blind to such a sight
An animate father, just pull his strings
but what difference do we make
the waves of rage and love so close
We couldn't keep them straight
No smile from life comes to us
a fear falls down like rain
run to hide deep in our room
our dreams might keep us sane
Thrashing and trembling outside the door
thunder comes crashing through
We could hear the passionate wrath out there
but perhaps we had no clue
A lifeless heart, left untouched
nor nurtured all those years
A pretty face to hide the memories
consumed by burning tears
The turn from love to hate to love
set our emotions on a spin
No matter if we gave him everything
His love we would never win
Despite those sudden fits of anger
or his moments of utter shame
He just took more of his medicine
and found someone else to blame.

1998

Mom

Sometimes time moves slowly and sometimes it moves so fast
Often our worries are in the future, though we are living in the past
There have been uncommon struggles, that we have somehow made it
through
So many times, I have been lonely, and I would think of you
There are always little mysteries, and some still are yet to be told
You are a part of each of mine, as each day my life unfolds
Without the caring heart within you, and the special love you show
I would dare not take another breath and life would cease to grow
I have wasted precious moments, and I have hurt the ones I love
Every night I say a prayer for help from Him above
For I never want to lose you, inside, my love is deep and strong
With you always in my heart, I try to right my wrongs
Sometimes it's hard to tell you, what my soul knows it feels
Because you are the one true thing in this crazy hand life deals
You will always have a special place inside of my heart
this poem is a part of me, though not much, it is a start
The words all seem so simple, just know that they are true
You mean the world and more to me Mom...
I love you.

Simple Moments

Just before my dreams consume me
and my eyes have yet to sleep
I think of something simple
that my dreams will surely keep
My breath slows and it calms me
and my eyes close to the night
A small spark guides me silently
with a warm and soothing light
When in my dreams, I see you
as an angel, you are there
To wash away my heartaches
and your special gifts, you share
My body forgets all the pain
and the memories become clear
In my dreams, you understand me
and give me comfort from my fears.
When I wake up in my wonder
remembering the sweetest smile
I dare to close my eyes once more
and dream for just awhile.

Inspiration

There is a future in the distance
sometimes it's hard to see
But I know that it's out there somewhere
because the dream's inside of me

Time often feels so endless
as it never stops or slows
But there is a wish I am wishing
and I'm watching as it grows

I cannot reach out to grab it
but I know that it waits
as time moves on so quickly
I just hope I'm not too late

I can see the dream I'm dreaming
right before my eyes
I know that I can catch it
if it takes a million tries

Always Me

So it's always me
Ha!! I didn't know
Is that what forced
you to go?
Wouldn't blame you
look at me
I'm nowhere near
where I should be
Stuck somewhere
in the past
And expecting anything
good could last
No worrying here
my tears are in vain
Wish I was anywhere
this life is mundane
Who really wants
to understand
I wouldn't want
to touch my hand

It's all fucked up
as it should be
I never feel
that's just me
So why the crying
why the pain?
Why feel at all
my life is plain
No reason to be here
no friend to me
I don't blame you
it's all I see
I want to throw
myself away
But I am stuck
and with me I stay
Maybe one day
I'll be someone
but for the moment
what's done is done

At The Bar

She hadn't even given him a second glance
a couple of beers between two friends
and now, she thought she might give him a chance
see if he's different, it all depends

She hadn't realized her hand was on his leg
and his mouth was warm on hers
And her blood raced and for his touch she begged
and the sweet taste of him was hers

She felt his touch and it felt so real
She hadn't remembered how good it could be
He gave her a reason to want to feel
her made her, unknowingly, be set free

And she didn't want to ever let go
for fear if she did, it all would end
But he did let go and love is so
and she waits for him to come again.

For Sean 12/9/99

Jesus

Something inside of me is dying to cry out and say something
there is a moment in time, missing inside of me...and my soul tries to
recall it
What could be missing, to make my entire life seem useless and empty
There must be so much more, where do I look? Where do I search?
What am I in Search of?
I remember this search I took some years ago
It was my search for self, for love, for life...for understanding.
I found my way, my fulfillment
through an eternal love for life and for others, through prayers
I felt freedom from pain and loss of material things...I learned
Eternal love purified my entire body, I felt clean and clear in my mind
Love flowed through me.
Smiles and songs where heartfelt and constant
Where did I go wrong? When did I lose sight of it?
I need His love Like I have never needed anything...Jesus.

During my very religious time...when I felt like Jesus had left me.

Good-byes

There is comfort in not knowing
what tomorrow's day will bring
and there is adventure in loving
though when it bites it stings

And there is humor in a simple joke
and a beauty in his eyes
just as there is a sorrow when
someone close to you has died

And even though I may not be there
when the morning nears
I promise one thing to you for always
it's never goodbye without tears.

You

You can see me
though I am not there
and you can speak to me
and never know I care
Because you cannot read me
and you would never ask
To even get to know me
might seem an endless task
But, oh, how I could love you
if you really want to know
I could share so many secrets
but instead you turn to go
And I could give you something
that I know you've never had
For the love I carry with me
might change those eyes so sad.

Nothing Love

Why will you not answer me
when so many nights I've called
when I've asked you if I matter
each time you have stalled

This only makes me hopeless
and inside I feel so small
and when I try to help you
then I take the fall

But still I feel these things inside
that keep me hanging on
and though sometimes I think you like me
right now the feeling's gone

For I need somebody
who will love me in such a way
that I can't make it through the hours
not knowing if he loves me through the days

And I will always have a place here
that I reserve especially for you
So when you think you can love me
then I will love you too.

Gone Away

the night is bitter in my memory
of the one who has gone away
I thought we'd have forever
but now he's gone today
And yesterday I was peaceful
for I knew that he was well
but yesterday left with the light
and now tomorrow will never tell
How empty all the nights are
when I lay here all alone
I never realized what he meant
until I was left here on my own
No one to reach out for comfort
from the fears I feel inside
No one there to love me now
the earth swallows me up to hide
I cannot stop the tears tonight
for I remember so well, his face
I remember how I felt so happy
when he filled this empty space
But someone took the one I love
because they simply didn't care
and now I feel I'm dying
because it just isn't fair
He was my hero
through the bitter nights so cold
he was the one who warmed me
and I had his love to hold
So why must he be taken
and I am left here all alone
I would have told him everything
if I could have known.

I Heard It All

I heard it all
in the words you didn't say
I heard the anger
when you turned and walked away

I saw it crumble
when you didn't look me in the eye
I saw the pain
when I found your words, were lies

I felt myself tremble
when you told me we were through
I felt heartache
when I knew I had lost you

I gave it all
for I never saw the truth
I gave my soul
until I had the proof

I left it all
and I found a new start
I left you behind
but I left you my heart.

Me

Do you really think you know me
or am I what you make of me?
Do I make you feel important
or just someone you'd like to be?
Do I give you any reason
to keep loving me this way
Or do you want to turn from me
just turn and walk away?
Am I the one you wanted
am I who you thought I was
Please don't say you stay here
and your reason's just because
do you think you can change me
or do you like who I am
Do you keep me cause you're lonely
or do you really give a damn?
Am I your latest project
and you think you're helping me?
Do you want to mold and shape me
because I am just what you see
Do you want to use me
until you find a better one
Do you want to keep me on a string
and think it hurts no one?
Do you think I may be different
because sometimes it's not so clear
I cannot be more than who I am
and you can't change the one who's here
For I am me and that is all
I can't change for anyone
I love you just the way you are
will you love me, or will you run?

A Vision

Another hour and another place
forgotten memories, forgotten face
She stands alone, she stands free
no one's for sure who she could be
A mysterious smile, a mysterious way
a dark and a light side to each day
A beautiful shadow of what's wrong and right
she's gone in morning, and alive by night
A haze of confusion, but we play the game
living without her is not the same
She spins in our thoughts and chases our fears
she holds us in comfort and dries our tears
Denied by the world, she saved our souls
she mended the wounds, she played out the roles
She gave us inspiration through turmoil and pain
now that she's gone things just aren't the same.

John

I remember how beautiful
you always saw the world
and how nothing ever changed
your outlook on life
and I remember how inspired I
was
when I saw how happy you were
and how you made anyone who
was down
smile even if it was only for a
moment
And I think I have never met
anyone
quite as wonderful as you
and I guess I thought I'd have
time to tell you
but I didn't know our times
were few
I know that if you could be here
I think you might be proud
of the way I have done things
since your candle burned out
I didn't know how to lose you
so I just pretended you were
here
I found you lying in your bed
and all your skin was blue
And I turned to my sister
and I think Daniel was there too
and I told them :guys, he's
dead"
and I felt sick inside.
And I couldn't believe the
words I'd said
and I told myself it was a lie
because you were happy and fun

and so good to me
and then in a few hours you
were gone
And I could never forget that
moment
when I saw you lying there
you seemed so peaceful and so
alone
but I knew you would have
someone to take care of you
For even if you were in Heaven
and not here with me and your
friends
you had a way with others
and would be ok anywhere
But I just want to tell you now
what I forgot to say back then
because I thought I had more
time with you
but I guess I really didn't
I love you for the friend you
were
and the friend you still are now
You are always alive in my heart
and we all miss you and love
you...we always did...Sorry John

Inside of Me

The purest form I ever saw
a ray of light so blind to all
She came so quickly and so fast
we knew this innocence would not last
so plain and simple, as she could be
she was the angel inside of me
A broken wing she shall not fly
no questions asked, no reason why
a hope, a vision...this she gave
for our lives she longed to save
A beautiful smile and sparkling eyes
she keeps in silence all her cries
To give a world what she can
to put her spirit into the soul of man
such subtle truth in her word
listen close to what is heard
she came along and changed our place
she came a shadow with no face
just a warmth I can't explain
washed away with the rain.

Little Girl

This little girl who lives inside
She turns her face and runs to hide.
Though in my sleep she begins to show
That she's been hurt and there's much to know.
A touch or a feeling she can't understand.
A memory awakens and she gives me her hand.
No longer alone in her fear and pain
No longer a victim to how she was trained.
She cries on my pillow and it burns in my heart.
Can't ever leave her or she'd break apart.
So together we'll walk through her path of fears,
And love will replace all of her questioning tears

Whatever it Was

what dreams may come I'll never know
sometimes I walk this world alone
I have some friends, though sometimes they're few
and tonight it's me...for where are you

no difference in the way I am
but see I just don't give a damn
for this is me, messed up and all
don't worry for me, I'll take the fall

too blind to see the love's not true
because I always wanted to feel for you
so let it be the way it is
let me be this...for this last kiss

the one who would be anything
who ever knew the pain it brings
if it made you believe in me
then that was all it was to be

no more me, for I am in you
you used me up, I had no clue
that you would run and turn your face
gone all at once, you left this place

left me forever, so I am alone
no whispers of the past, I wait at the phone
no pushing for more than I could be
I pushed so hard you walked from me

but such is life, the story goes
I am the only one who knows
so live and love as you have done
for once we were two into one.

Times

dusty pictures, in some old chest
remembered times, weren't they the best?
Old days forgotten somewhere in time
gone to dust and turned to crime

old pieces of our younger days
youthful looks in yearbooks always stay
treasures forgotten with troubled life
I have a job, you've got a wife

no more gifts for us to share
weren't we such a special pair
but gone forever are the dreams
for life back then has past it seems

but to the memories, I shall hold
to all the love that was untold
and in these eyes, so clear and green
like the rarest emerald you have ever seen

look closely into the depths within
see all the words that can't begin
and take the hand that reaches to you
you'll dream again and I will too

So They'll Love Me

a desperate cry into the darkness
an echo lost for miles
a distance from the trust in life
a walk through many trials
a shaken memory in her head
a deep wound she cannot heal
a shattered dream all around her
and she can't remember how to
feel
she uses what she knows she has
what she doesn't feel she needs
she gives her body to the fire
and the wounds begin to bleed
can't feel what love is
can't get close enough to touch
can't ever let them get too close
because she knows it hurts too
much
another driven anger
she knows not from where it
comes
another fury in her soul
sometimes she feels so dumb
what is love anyway
is it really all they say
no one ever said I love you
and is still around today

some left with out a warning
and some they chose to cheat
some they lied and carried on
but it always showed defeat
some they said they loved her
and others never lied
some they said she was
everything
but not one ever really tried
it all played out just like a game
one she could not win
so when the feeling turned to
fear
she turned her life to sin
at least this way she didn't feel
and she didn't have to lie
she told them all why they were
there
so they wouldn't try to pry
of course it left her with a lot of
guilt
and nothing else to give
but she didn't know how to love
them
and it was the only way she
knew to live

Jealousy

so empty inside is the jealous heart
who trusts no one because of insecurity
so alone is the soul who cannot trust
for there is no one hurting but you

so afraid is the one who cannot reach out
because of pain from their past
so closed to the world of life is the spirit
who cannot laugh along with the one she despises

Time runs wild on and on
it doesn't stop for the one who cries
jealous hearts are so alone and empty
for those souls only hurt themselves.

Who Am I?

I stand here, naked and frail
showing you my scars, my pain, my tears
I curl up here on the floor
and wonder if my fears are because of you
or if they are because of man himself
I am here before you
showing you all of me, opening my soul
here for you...wondering what do you see?
Do you want only what you see in clothing
in make up, in jewelry...
do you want the dirt and the tragedy, the sin and the regret?
do you see me, or do you not see me at all
I stand here naked and alone, unprotected
will you warm me and accept me...or am I just a body
made for sin, and not a soul and a heart with pain and tears
and love and life inside of me
standing before you
who am I?

Depths of Me

the depths of me are seen by few
for they never take the time
sometimes I know what they think of me
and their thoughts to me are crimes

the smaller things that make me up
seem to get misplaced somewhere
and the body and the mind are separate
but to me it's just not fair

for he comes to me in my dreams
wanting to love me more each day
but in my heart I know the truth
he comes in and out but never stays

for he sees me as something else
something I could never be
he loves what I can give him
but loves nothing about me

And what in life is ever fair
he knows not where I've been
all he knows is my body is good for something
all he sees in me is sin

Your Love Feels

I wake each morning and I see you there
and I know in that instance just how much I care
for each breath that you take, you share with me
and each smile you give, says we're meant to be

And the moments when time must keep us apart
forever, your love burns deep in my heart
And I know when I cry you wipe the tears away
you make my life worth living each day

I long for the nights when I am in your arms
when you comfort and hold me and keep me from harm
I hold tight to your picture and that special look
and how when I was frightened, you held me, no matter how long it took

You are my reason and I am your rhyme
we fill the gaps between your heart and mine
I love you each morning and I love you each night
For only you, my love, make me feel so right.

He Knows You

Breathe a little deeper
and it will help you to think clear
for I know the confusion
and the love for him, you fear

Say the words, unspoken
that you mean for him to hear
For through you he will understand
and you will see he is near

Drop a kiss upon his pillow
whisper softly in his ear
Show him what you're feeling
for he is standing here

Brush his hair back from his face
and see him in the light
Let him feel the love you have
for he already knows it's right

Reach out and take his hand now
and softly look him in the eye
Tell him how you need him
and you just don't know why

Wrap your arms around him
and fight that fear inside
the trembling isn't bad you see
if you tell him, it will subside

I know the words you long to speak
and I think he hears them too
Say the words and you will see
that this man's in love with you.

Love's Memories

a whisper from so far away
lost in time, love slips this day
into some darkness she had known
far from here her dreams have flown

she feels the pain burn her inside
she can't escape the tears she's cried
So far gone slipped all the nights
a cloud of dust in the light

Forever broken, loving his face
forever a memory she cannot erase
she's forgiven his troubles, but they have left scars
she tries to go on, though it hasn't worked out so far

Alone and crying, she has no place to turn
love is a game, in which, she'll never learn
and for all of the heartache, she would give once again
to love another, and feel something within

for throughout the years, she has been left cold
never had anything solid on which she could hold
She longs for the touch of someone who will care
There are so many moments that she hopes to share

And if you look to her smile and you see in her eyes
you could feel the emotion that she tries to disguise
But somewhere inside of her, there is a heart
that burns with a love, she longs to start.

Untitled

so many nights I have thought about
the ways I could love you
but in the light of day I turn away
knowing it can't be true
I see you there each morning
and throughout my days and nights
I think of what I want so much
and what is taken at first light
You never whisper anything
never show anything for me
you keep it hidden well or else
you do not want this to be
I need so many things from life
but I feel this way for you
and I feel so confused these days
for all the things you do
you never try and call me
and you keep any thoughts of me on guard
you don't let me know what you see
sometimes it seems so hard
to feel a certain feeling
but be forced to hold it in
I don't understand the reasons
I don't know where I've been
but I never remembered it being so hard
to feel love for anyone
but I think you hide the things you feel
somewhere beneath the sun
I can hardly keep it
all inside of my mind
I think about you all the time
but I seem stuck or left behind
is it because it has been so long
and I know not what to do
I know I can do something
to show what I feel for you

"The world is a dangerous place to live, not because of evil people, but because of people who see evil and yet stand by and do nothing." --Albert Einstein

Drifting

drifting along life's endless ocean
forgotten, it seems, by the world
A quiet night dances upon the waters
the waves, a dancer, she endlessly twirls
The moon staring into the night
as if it would like to say something
loneliness offers the poor man a ride
Nothing, is all he's allowed to bring
So softly tears fill up this pool
of lost loves that still hold on
and so clear we see the foolish hearts
they don't see that love has gone
the colorful life they try to give
to the creatures in the lake
not a lie, but just their dreams
and his lonely life, they long to take
free as the gulls that fly above the seas
and eat right from another's hand
able to shine in the night skies
and rest in fields of unknown lands
For life holds every moment sacred
Loneliness only a part of this sea
Life is like the ocean baby
like your soul is to me.

I Wished For You

I Wished for you when you were gone
upon stars so bright, through nights so long
I prayed to my angel, that I'd find a way
to give you my love, and somehow you'd stay
Somehow my dreams have drifted someplace
as life took a turn, time runs some race
and my feet stumble, and forget how to run
blinded by trouble, searching for the sun
But my heart still holds tightly to the magic in me
that believes in you always, knowing someday you'll see
Forever a promise I once made to you
through the grayest of skies, my words would be true
And no matter the distance or the times left between
you are thought of with love, you'll be kept in my dream.

In Her Soul

forbidden dreams, her fantasy
so kept within her soul
a destiny she'd never know
she'd never be quite whole

despite the painful memories
and all the shadowed faces
she stepped away from the safety net
to travel to other places

so alone in her room she drifted
far from where her fears would lay
to a jeweled city, unspoken tongues
where her heart was safe to stay

the soul still held a spark of life
that no one ever thought to see
inside her body, she held the love
that she knew could set her free.

All In My Way

today is the beginning
of not just a brand new day
but of the life that I could have
if I am pleasant in what I do and say

I know that some are angered
and others are having trouble at home
but a smile could make a difference
if taken everywhere I roam

I don't think it's much trouble
to be nice and lend a hand
because sometimes it's all somebody needs
is for someone to understand

And it feels so good to know that
I have kept someone from feeling sad
because I may have been the only
bit of sunshine that they've had

Untitled

I miss you with every breath I take
oh the difference that you make
so filled inside with love for you
sometimes it feels as though it can't be true
For so long, I was afraid to say
that I had felt this way
but just one life I have to live
and to you, my love I long to give
I dream of days when you are here
and I can share this love, I hold so near
for ever I believe in you
and I am hoping you will feel it too
Some say I'm crazy for all of this
but one night with you I wouldn't miss
you fill my soul so it overflows
you understand, you know things no one else knows
God this never comes out quite right
to read this now, I'd say it bites
I try to get the words out clear
but I can only show you...when you're here
Well I suppose you know what I want to say
with us it's always been that way
So the only thing left for me to do
is simply tell you that I love you.

Distance Love

miles away, over the seas
I still feel you inside of me
nothing here could ever replace
the love I hold, in some special place
I'd wait forever though some don't understand
to hold you close to me, it's not as I planned
but you have become so much more than they know
I take your words with me, wherever I go
No one has ever made me feel as you do
and I hope that somehow I make you feel that way too
For all the emotion I feel at the thought
of feeling such love, it won't be forgot
for ever and always, I hold you in here
part of this soul, my heart holds no fear
I trust you as I haven't trusted in years
I give you my love, my heart and my tears
for only you deserve such a place in my heart
for only you know what we both long to start
and whatever is said about how we both feel
no matter this distance, I love you still.

Where Do I Begin

I can't begin to tell you the ache I feel inside
I couldn't start to show it so inside of me it hides
I wouldn't know the words that could tell you what I feel
I might say it harshly as these pains, I feel, could kill
But I wouldn't like to hurt you just because love is confused
Or even tell you I am broken, your words made me feel used
And if your doubts are bigger then all this love I've shown
then I don't think my pleading would fix the way our love has grown
But don't try to run and hold me just because you see my tears
because it's all a part of loving I have felt it through the years
God, see I don't want to lose you but it all comes out that way
see I'm trying to say you hurt me still I do want you to stay
But not if you are doubting what's between your heart and mine
you see I need a strong love not one that walks that fine line
because I love you true and simply from the deepest part of my soul
but I won't force that feeling if I don't make your life whole
See I love the pleasures but I know it comes with pain
but I'll only take the hurt, you see if your love is pure and plain
and if you somehow doubt me and don't believe these words I say
all I know is that I say them true for that's the only way
Baby, I do love you but you're confused by this, I fear
it's not some game I play for fun my intentions should be clear
I'll love you, no expectations for the man that I have seen
no more than what you give to me just for YOU, is what I mean.

It Would Always Be

I thought it would last forever
I thought we would always be
I suppose it's just this foolish heart
that was too blind to see
I'm sorry that I doubted
but to me the words were clear
I wanted to believe in you
but I was caught up in my fear
But I guess that I deserve this
though tonight I'll think and cry
wondering how it went this way
but I guess we didn't try
And maybe it was just too wrong
though I know it felt so right
But I'll go on and live this life
if I can make it through this night

Rain

it begins softly as if a whisper in your ear
slowly and methodically as if to place you in a trance
To understand it's language you must feel it in your soul
it might leave swiftly, this is your chance

It drowns the hurried and hasty world
and makes you see things careful and true
It blinds the sight of those who never rest
to wash within it, this makes for a purer you

But sometimes we take these things for granted
we don't see the beauty in the things of life
There is a passion and a fury in it's coming
but we blind it with our pain and our strife

Feel it in the palm of your hands
as it is cool yet refreshingly nice
It won't harm you if you would only pay attention
but in our hurry we just don't think twice

The Girl I Used To Be

I wake to light each morning
and for a moment a smile finds my face
before I feel this sadness
and long to leave this place

I search through my closet
what secrets will I find
Choose which mask to wear today
to disguise what's on my mind

A laugh and a pretty smile
hide all my guilt and shame
what looks back in the mirror
doesn't like this game

So much anger and endless crying
so much disgust for what I see
can't find the strength to reveal
the girl I used to be

Live Your Dream

search the moon, make a dream
invent your own night sky
Draw the stars, see how they shine
make a wish and watch it fly

Drift inside the unknown clouds
and find inspiration where there's doubt
Sing to the angels who turn to see
what such love could be about

Gently reach out the hand of comfort
to the soul that's feeling used
Give a hug to a child who's innocence
has been left alone and abused

And never give up the dreams you keep
no matter how deep inside they hide
one day with hopes and wishes
they won't be locked inside

And if you'd like to share them
well baby I would volunteer
To share forever and your dreams
for my heart will keep you near.

Eternal

there is distance and space between our lives
but remember our hearts still beat in time
Some say to love someone so far away
how that pain must be a crime

Each night when my sun is setting
I know yours has just begun
So I look to heaven, wish on a star
just before my day is done

And though there are miles between us
still with faith, I'll hold you near
Though at times, it feels so hopeless
I know someday you will be here

And my dawn will be the same for you
and my days and nights will be as yours
Our sunsets and our mountains, the same
we'll sleep on the same shores

And it is for these days I will wait
and for these feelings I'll hold on
Through my lifetime and Eternity
Forever my love will go on

I'll Go On

I thought it would last forever
I thought we would always be
I suppose it's just this foolish heart
that was too blind to see

I'm sorry that I doubted
but to me the words were clear
I wanted to believe in you
but I was caught up in my fear

But I guess that I deserve this
though tonight I'll think and cry
wondering how it went this way
but I guess we didn't try

And maybe it was just too wrong
though I know it felt so right
But I'll go on and live this life
if I can make it through this night

I Learned

I learned how to love, when I was alone
I learned to be strong, when I was weak, on my own
I learned how to feel, when I was untouched
I learned to believe, when the thieves took too much
I learned to accept, when life was unfair
I learned understanding, from those who didn't care
I learned to laugh, from the tears that I cried
I learned about honesty, from those who have lied
I learned understanding, from being left in the cold
I learned to surrender from just growing old
I learned how to feel, without being touched
from longing to love, and losing so much
I learned how to smile, and mask the frowns
I learned true heartache from watching the clowns
I learned what true life is, from losing it all
I lived and I learned this, from taking the fall.

What Matters

It doesn't interest me if you are beautiful, but do you find beauty in life.
Do you wish to stand atop the tallest mountain and declare your love of
it?

It does not interest me whether or not you have all the money of the
world
What interests me is whether or not you would give away your last dollar
to help a hungry child.

It doesn't matter to me that you have falsified love to many women
what I wonder is have you been blessed with knowing love at all

My eyes do not see around you, your clothes, your style or your words
My eyes see into you, the wonder and amazement that only a true love
might bring

It does not interest me if you would give up all you have known to love
and be with me..
just that you would stay the night and hold me close to you, is enough.

It doesn't matter at all to me that you have seen pain and tragedy,
but rather that you have become stronger and more understanding of the
pains others face each day because of that.

It does not matter to me that I must be lonely for a while without you,
what matters is that you will one day be here with me...because I love
you.

Untitled

When all the world is sleeping
When the day has said goodnight
And the stars shine bright upon us
And protect us in their light
Then the evening brings a memory
Remembered only in the deepest soul
And the times of constant changing
Settle in the hopes someone once stole
Before the dream of something better
Could form itself in our mind
First we learned life's greatest lesson
The one true thing our hearts must find
So softly love enters our lifetime
Quietly held by our fragile hands
Knowing nothing of the feelings
Still hoping someone understands
Love drifts in and out as a current
As a wave upon the seas
Sometimes soft and rhythmic
Sometimes rough as the tides can be
And yet we learned to hold it
Safely sheltered from the pain
Though it's clear how love can hurt us
Still it's a need we can't explain
That thing we need so badly
It's the same something, that we fear
It pulls us through the hard times
And makes the winding road more clear
For without a love to believe in
What better thing to share
Love is the thread that binds us
And inspires us to care.

Untitled

Through Every Hour

Through every hour I spent in darkness

When I'd fight to find some light

Words unspoken, feelings that we knew

Helped me through the night

For every moment I felt hopeless

And the tears fell from my eyes

Shut tight to keep the ghosts away

Afraid of the goodbyes

I found you in those times I cried

Locked up inside my dreams

Knowing I could keep you close

When the rest isn't as it seems

For you are my strength in times

That I could not stand alone

And you made me believe in life

And I didn't have to feel this on my own

So even though you can't be close

Still inside my heart, you're near

And each day that passes, I surely know

That soon you will be here

And my arms, they wait for you

Hoping that you feel the same

Though it's strange that we have never met

Just two faceless names

I can't deny the feelings

That are surely racing through my veins

Trust that I will love you

When the sky brings the rains

I hope that you don't question

If the things I say to you are real

I know it may be hard to know for sure

But this is how I feel

I would wait for you forever

And share my self with you

I wouldn't take those things for granted

I only hope you know it's true

For the days I spend without you

I think of you throughout those days

Knowing time will bring us together

I only hope that you will stay.

And in the darker moments

When I wish that you were here

I simply think of many tomorrows

And I see my life quite clear

Could all the dreams I hope for

Become promises we'll keep

I know sometimes it seems I'm crazy

That I've fallen in too deep

But just know I miss you

And I know you'll understand

It's just that I know I need you

Even though it's not what I had planned

I never thought I would love again

I never even looked for this before

You feel from heaven into my heart

And I need look no more.

The Secrets That I Keep

Sometimes the darkness scares me
The silence lingers in the air
The night steals away the good dreams
Instead his face is there.

It often leaves me trembling
I'm left motionless with fear
Though it's all in my imagination
Still I see him there so clear.

And no matter how I try to ignore it
It's a memory I just can't bare
Every turn I make is guarded
Because I fear someone is there

So my nights go on forever
Endless even in my dreams
Every sound echoes through me
November takes over me, it seems

So if you wonder why it's morning
And still I have yet to sleep
It's all because of what's inside of me
The secrets that I keep.

Untitled

Too many nights are wasted
On the memories of bad times
And all the tears are senseless
And we accept the crimes

Love doesn't often last, you know
It's not written there in stone
It comes rushing in and carries us
But then one day you're all alone

Can't explain what makes those feelings
Cause our eyes to be so blind
Don't understand the heartaches
When that love is left behind

Only know for just one moment
A special part of you was shared
And you knew the best of life
For the chance at love, you dared.

We find patience through another
And we're inspired by the day
Knowing every breath we take
Our love will feel it in some way

For that is selflessness, you see
Something you learn through the trials
And for all the pains, the tears, the joys
These are lessons through the miles

So no time here is useless
No moment should be spared
No words of deceit ever spoken
Just remember all we've shared.

Floating In

I sit here feeling lonely
Wondering if one day maybe I'll find someone
Never sure if this is my destiny
And regretting my past, for what I've done

I can't take back the pain, you see
I can't erase those plots in time
I cannot mend the heart I broke
Nor fix the violent crime

Now they remain a part of me, I hide
But they still weigh down my heart and mind
I cannot find my place in life
I feel I've been left behind

Sometimes I feel like I'm floating
Not really living here at all
I want someone or to love just once
Before my life should fall.

It Would Bother Me

Does it bother you how you get picked on
Because it would bother me A great deal
She wondered, if it bothers her so
Why does she participate and not think of how I feel

Does it mean much to you when they hurt you
With their hurtful words and remarks
But she says those words as often
And thinks I can't hear them in the dark

Does it make you sad to fight for your self
When they say your point of view is wrong
But she laughs as much as the rest
They all have for so long

He Doesn't

It seems I've already lost him
Even though I haven't heard the words
It feels like what he wants to tell me
Is something I've already heard

Here I am trying to find a way
To tell his heart to love me
To find some link between us
So things could be as I want them to be

But the phone has already stopped
It's ringing, at least on my end
And the response is silence
To all the letters that I try to send

I don't think he sees me now
Not the way he did the first time
Love is always that same old game
Having no reason or rhyme

Wonder what he doesn't see in me
That I see in him so much
Is my heart too shallow or too deep
He doesn't burn with my touch

I think he's already gone
There's nothing in his eyes
He doesn't look inside of me now
All these feelings seem like lies

He doesn't notice me in the room
Like he did all those times before
He doesn't hurry to talk to me
He just doesn't want me anymore.

I'll Still Love You

Give me just one moment
I could make you understand
If I only had just one chance
None of this was planned
How I fell in love with you
Is a puzzle in my mind
But I never doubted how I felt
Though I didn't know the love I'd find.
It wasn't like I questioned
Whether it was right or wrong
I simply made the magic
Something for my whole life long
I promised you forever
I would always be there
I knew I'd love you always
So you'd know how much I care
So to tell me it's over
That it's time that you let go
The pain of my heart breaking
Oh you could never know
For everything within me
I have given it to you
You say this way is easier
Then you really have no clue
Because this love is endless
And I'm not going anywhere
I said I'd love you for your lifetime
So this is only fair
Don't deprive me of having
Even these last few years
To give to you my heart and soul
To share your pain and tears.
You know my words are spoken
And I hold them, they are true
If our forever cannot last that long
Still I will love you.

In His Hands

Starlit night, what do you see?
Is there life inside of me?
Along the path of twisted fate
Tell me are my dreams too late?

Drifting along a lonely sea
Hoping he'd find his way back to me
Still alone in the garden of despair
I wonder sometimes if he still cares

For he never came back, no one's here
He said goodbye, He made it all so clear
I realized for the first time, in years
How much I loved him, and then fell the tears

Moon shine in my dreams, in my soul
Replace this heart, make me whole
To remember the time when he loved me
And never forget, who I could be

You see, the love I gave had no doubt
He never understood, what it was about
Life and love, and along came pain
Like the warmth of sun, brings freezing rain

He is here, locked inside of me
I know somehow he will see
I placed my heart within his hands
Hoping one day he understands.

Jess Poem

Through every hour I spent in
darkness
When I'd fight to find some light
Words unspoken, feelings that we
knew
Helped me through the night

For every moment I felt hopeless
And the tears fell from my eyes
Shut tight to keep the ghosts away
Afraid of the good-byes

I found you in those times I cried
Locked up inside my dreams
Knowing I could keep you close
When the rest isn't as it seems

For you are my strength in times
That I could not stand alone
And you made me believe in life
And I didn't have to feel this on
my own

So even though you can't be close
Still inside my heart, you're near
And each day that passes, I surely
know
That soon you will be here

And my arms, they wait for you
Hoping that you feel the same
Though it's strange that we have
never met
Just two faceless names

I can't deny the feelings
That are surely racing through my
veins
Trust that I will love you
When the sky brings the rains

I hope that you don't question
If the things I say to you are real
I know it may be hard to know for
sure
But this is how I feel

I would wait for you forever
And share my self with you
I wouldn't take those things for
granted
I only hope you know it's true

For the days I spend without you
I think of you throughout those
days
Knowing time will bring us
together
I only hope that you will stay.

And in the darker moments
When I wish that you were here
I simply think of many tomorrows
And I see my life quite clear

Could all the dreams I hope for
Become promises we'll keep
I know sometimes it seems I'm
crazy
That I've fallen in too deep

But just know I miss you
And I know you'll understand
It's just that I know I need you
Even though it's not what I had
planned

I never thought I would love again
I never even looked for this before
You fell from heaven into my heart
And I need look no more.

Leave It Up To Fate

I just can't explain it
Still it burns me up inside
The weight of never knowing
All the feelings that I hide

The loss of my emotion
When we play kiss and tell
When secrets are the answer
And love is what we sell

Can't fight the moment
Or the need to be with you
A part of me is crying
But what else can I do

I feel I am competing
Even though you say it's not a game
If I love…then I will lose
But if I lie it's not the same

So do I stand to lose you
In this game of love and hate
And if I fight to have you
It's still left up to fate

Life Turns

Destiny has no straight path
It changes as it goes
Our lives are shaped by trials
Some that we never could let go

Life holds so many lessons
It gives us strength when we are weak
It holds our hearts and sets them free
And gives us the love that we seek

And sometimes it brings us heartache
And sometimes it burns with pain
It makes us struggle for a hand to hold
And gives shelter from the rain

At times it can be so uncertain
And we feel so misunderstood
But then other days we smile
And know it's ok…in ways we never thought it would

So it turns and there is sorrow
And then it turns and it's alright
Life doesn't have a pattern
Only daylight and night

But if we look a little closer
And see our selves a bit more clear
Life doesn't have to be so bad
As we look back upon the years

Life

4/27/01
11:49:43 PM

There aren't always answers
to the questions that run through our minds
That's part of life...to learn
by feeling...searching for what we need to find.

There isn't one right path
there isn't just one wrong turn
No two instances are alike
we all have so much to learn

We wouldn't know love if
we didn't have hate within
But how we use those emotions
is the key to how life begins

Sun can be warming and pure
as night can be dark and cold
or you can flip it inside out
and find comfort from what the night holds

You can look at a painting
full of bright colors...and see nothing
or you can see the feelings held there
the colors capture something.

you can wake in the morning
wishing to live out your dreams
but just remember that there's reality
things aren't as they seem.

Longing To Be

Longing to be
Who hides inside
Knowing it's there
Why does it hide?
Wanting to open
The door closed so tight
Pushing and pushing
To make it feel right
Never ignoring it
This feeling I feel
Let me love this moment
Knowing it's real
For in an instant
Today might rush on
Tomorrow may tell me
Forever he's gone
Leaving behind
Those painful days
Slipping from the hand
And drifting away
Leave my heart empty
Only words to replace
The rest of his love
Has been erased

Love Wants Forever

Dreams are only moments
Too hard for one to see
A means to lessen pain
That lasts in a fantasy

Pictures capture precious things
Bring back a forgotten face
A friend you've said good-bye to
But remains forever there someplace

A tear holds many secrets
Of what the heart forgets to tell
Filled with the words we've lost
After the fires pale

A smile masks her heartache
And disguises the loss she feels
It covers the wounds with make-up
Though those scars have yet to heal

A laugh seems like a blessing
As it hides behind it's fear
As love wants forever
She would die to make it clear

Maybe This Time

Sometimes I can't even think straight
There's just so much going on inside
And sometimes I wonder if any of this is real
Don't know how much to show or how much to hide

There were times before when I wondered
Times when I really thought you cared
I didn't know if it would really last
But then I remember all the things I shared

I hoped you'd stay around
Never knowing how to hide what I feel
Knowing it had to be a secret
Made me unsure if it was real

But I always knew there was something
Something I had seen long ago
I wanted to tell you months before
But I couldn't let you know

Second chances are one in a million
You see, there are games I don't like to play
But we never got the chance to start
So maybe this time you'll stay

Moving On

There are times I've looked back on my life
And been amazed by the things I've seen
There must be a lot of people out there
Who read this and know exactly what I mean

It's funny how in that moment
I would wish it all to end
Or give anything to forget the broken heart
That somehow along the way, would mend

And there were times I sat alone
Feeling so empty inside…my soul would cry
And I'd ask the same question as the rest of you
Receiving no answer to that question…"Why?"

But today when I look back on my life
I don't see anything I would regret
And I know I have a lot more learning to do
Because the world isn't through with me yet

But my life is beautiful in all its faults
Because I have become stronger from those trials
And I have many things to laugh about and people to thank
For being part of who I am, even if only for a little while

Sometimes I think back and wonder
Where all the years have gone
But I smile knowing I'll always remember
Although my life has moved on.

Not That Way

I feel for him
So much
So many things he's done for me
He has no clue
He understand me
But he doesn't know I long to lay beside him
To be with him
When I think of him
I feel the warmth of his skin
His breath on my neck
His touch making me lose control
And lose my fear
This man shows me love
Like I haven't known
Makes me feel special, important
I want so to draw him into me
To hold him
Forever
To kiss him and to let this show
How I feel
How I always want to be near
And feel the way he makes me feel
His arms wrapped around me
While we sleep
Shows me he doesn't want me to go
He wants me to stay there
It isn't just for one night
My lips tremble when I kiss him
When I dream of him
How I want him to know
But this man who loves me
Who makes me feel so good inside
Who makes me love again
He doesn't know...
He just doesn't love me
Not that way.

Once Again

Here I am once again. All I can
Think about is you. With this ever present longing
I just can't explain. I feel it so
Deeply within my soul that I want to scream
Or perhaps cry.
Because while I have already found you to be amazingly
Beautiful. While I have already
Known you in such a way that I could
Never explain to anyone. I also know
I could never call you mine.
Possibly you want more from a woman.
Maybe it's me, maybe it's you.
I'm tormented with love for you.
Sometimes even jealous that you can love me so much
Be such a friend to me, yet love me so little in the same
Breath.
Here I am once again, in my loneliness. Wishing...
Wanting and longing to share my dream with
You.

One

He stirs something
Inside of me
Something no one else
Ever could
He awakens a part
Of me
I thought no one
Ever would
Every word he spoke
Still lingers
And I long to feel
His touch
Every breath he takes
Runs through me
No one has ever meant
So much
He is the light that guides
my dream
for he believes so much
in me

He's my reason he's my
Everything
He's my eyes so I
Can see
He gives my life
It's reason
He's my warmth when
There is rain
He lifts me above
The emptiness
He kisses away
My pain.
One man who lives
Forever
Who helped my life
To start
In this secret world
I've found
One soul who holds
My heart

Poem

Can't stop the heat
That burns me up inside
The rushing of the moment
When the need, I cannot hide

Don't want to lose it
The warmth of his skin
The loss of control I have
When he finally lets me in

Such passion never known
Alive by his touch
His lips upon my lips
Leaves me trembling so much

Hands that draw me in
Holding me so near
Longing for his love tonight
Want to feel this fear

Heart upon his heart
Breath drawn into my soul
The moment takes me over
His love takes control

Good bye to the morning
His arms there when I wake
And know I have to leave him
The bittersweet one I forsake

The Questions

Gold and silver thread she holds
As though it keeps her from falling
Yet what is so precious in this thread
As if it's her destiny calling

She says her hands are different
Old or not so sensitive now
And her eyes aren't as green as before
And she wonders how

Could the light have turned darker
And the bright white turned gray
And her eyes lost the sunshine
And night taken the day

What made the moment
Turn to ashes and dust
Why did her heart become
Tarnished with rust

What makes life so endless
And why do we live on
When their hands have closed up
And the love now has gone

Questions

In my head I keep these questions
They play over and over in my mind
I wonder if I'm pushing him
And wonder about the things I've left behind

I don't remember how to do this
How to give and still hold back
How to share the secrets inside of me
Without getting too off track

How do I know when to be silent
When the words may be too much
How do I control the aching
When I long to feel his touch

What is too fast for me
Or what might make him turn away
I just want to hold on to this
How do I make him stay?

Because I think about the moments
When I'm sitting here alone
And I know that I could love him
Because he's more than I've ever known

And I wonder if my longing
May not be what he needs
But I want so much to love him
For the first time my soul feels free

So I question am I certain
And every day I want him more
So though there is confusion
I know he's worth waiting for.

Saying Goodbye

I don't know how to forget someone
Who touched my life in such a way
A friend who chose to listen
When thoughts clouded up my day
How do I go on without thinking
How lonely it is now that he's gone
How do I spend this moment
And make my life go on?
The pain burns in me so deeply
And the ache is hard to bare
The whole world just feels empty
Knowing he's not there
I know he lived a good life
But did he know he made mine that way too
Did he know how much I loved him
I hope he had a clue
Because I can't remember if I told him
I don't know if it was clear
That he brought out the best in me
Through the past two years
How do I say goodbye to him
And smile through my tears
How do I let him go so fast
How do I tame these fears
I only hope he knew me
Well enough to know he's missed
And I hope that he is safe now
I hope God grants him that final wish
He will be remembered
For the good inside his heart
I guess I have to say goodbye now
Though in ways, we'll never part.

Silent In This Crowded House

Silent in this crowded house
I have only thoughts of you
Alone in a busy world
This is all I want to do

Different lives, alone tonight
I see nothing through these eyes
Deep in a soul that's haunted
Through dreams, this time she cries

All those tears, that never fell
Finding somewhere else to sleep
Away from the world, hiding
All those secrets that she keeps

Beneath her foot, a solid earth
Bound to it by her pain
Across the miles of emptiness
Throughout the land of rain

She knows she's lost the one
Who lives inside her still
The one she'll love forever
He'll never understand how she feels

The Mask

Beneath the masks of unknown faces
Through the many trials still unseen
Walking through the ghosts of our pasts
Wondering simply, what does life mean?

Trying not to show the anger
Trying to hide a pain we know too well
Hoping they think we are the strong ones
And that our sorrows they cannot tell

But it all grows so within us
That we fight how our secrets burn inside
It's too hard to try and explain it
To big for us to try and hide

For life is full of lessons
Some too tearful to endure
All we have is the hope that someone knows
Understands…or might have a cure.

Might have an ear for to listen
Might have arms to wrap around
Or maybe a hand to hold…a smile
An understanding…without a sound.

A friend who doesn't push you
One who doesn't need to ask
Because you both have been there
She knows who hides beneath your mask.

The Night's Embrace

When darkness comes to steal this light
That keeps the fears away
I stumble down it's gravel road
Just trying to find my way

I hold the tears back, wearily
When I'm held in the night's embrace
Shut my eyes and try to dream
I'm in another place

Turning 'round in circles
A cycle I just can't break
Reaching out in blindness
Hoping something stirs me to wake

Drifting through a moment
I have drifted through before
Replaying old pains in my mind
Don't want to see this anymore

But it's just another flashback
Another time and another place
Another year that passed in silence
Just one more night that I must face

May 9, 2001

There Is

There's a difference in the way he smiles
It takes my breath away
There's a knowing when he looks at me
That words could not explain

There's a distance still between us
But my heart holds him near
There's a power that's connecting us
Until he can be here

I know the heart has reasons
That reason just can't understand
I can't explain this road I've chosen
But he holds my love in his hands

And there's a knowing in not knowing
What tomorrow's light will bring
Because I know that if he wasn't here
My life wouldn't mean a thing

I'd give away a thousand dreams
Just to see his smile
I'd promise forever, I'd give it all
To love him for awhile.

There is a silence that is understood
When our souls speak to our hearts
There is nothing better in this life
Then what we long to start.

When All The World Is Sleeping

When all the world is sleeping
When the day has said goodnight
And the stars shine bright upon us
And protect us in their light
Then the evening brings a memory
Remembered only in the deepest soul
And the times of constant changing
Settle in the hopes someone once stole
Before the dream of something better
Could form itself in our mind
First we learned life's greatest lesson
The one true thing our hearts must find
So softly love enters our lifetime
Quietly held by our fragile hands
Knowing nothing of the feelings
Still hoping someone understands
Love drifts in and out as a current
As a wave upon the seas
Sometimes soft and rhythmic
Sometimes rough as the tides can be
And yet we learned to hold it
Safely sheltered from the pain
Though it's clear how love can hurt us
Still it's a need we can't explain
That thing we need so badly
It's the same something, that we fear
It pulls us through the hard times
And makes the winding road more clear
For without a love to believe in
What better thing to share
Love is the thread that binds us
And inspires us to care.

Untitled

Late nights, empty lives
Lost souls, within nothing grows
Broken promises, still as time
Forgotten girl, no one knows.

Silent crying, eyes of coal
Beneath the covers, thin disguise
They laughed behind her
She hears their lies.

So why do they talk so mean?
And think she's a fool?
To cover the truth about themselves
So others might think they're cool.

But she knows herself well enough
To walk away with nothing to hide
Because one thing they can't steal
Is the respect she holds inside.

Untitled

Silent one, her eyes seem gray
Lost in her moment, no words to say
They laugh behind her, she hears his name
She doesn't take part in the rumors and games

Promises made, some years ago
Will he break them, she just doesn't know.
One way in life, and she puts on her mask.
Avoiding the questions they all want to ask.

Hidden within her, kept close to her heart
She thinks of the one – something she longs to start.
Afraid she's starting it off all wrong
She knows she wants him, it's just been so long.

Untitled

I wish you knew the feelings
That have consumed me inside
It's something I've been missing
And now it's hard to hide.

I keep thinking about you
Hoping I will see you again
Waiting nearly all my life
I wonder where you've been

I hope it's not saying too much
I feel so many things for you
But I can't hold it all inside
Because to myself, I must be true.

I'm still unsure how you feel
Or what you see in me
But, God, I must be lucky
For whatever it is you see.

Untitled

There's something rushing through me
And it's so hard to explain
All these years, going by so fast
Through deserted roads and icy rains

I struggled with my future
Had to break free from my past
So maybe I could find somebody
And feel like it might last.

I learned how to walk with patience
And how to share a part of me
To make this world I live in
The kind that it should be.

And now that I've grown stronger
And my truth has made me free
I think I've found somebody
And I hope that he's found me.

Untitled

All the tears and sadness
I see it every day
I wonder if I spoke to them
Would it help them in some way.

I have felt what they are feeling
I know the things they hide
Afraid others won't accept
The person locked inside

Kind words were never spoken
And so they never knew
We always assume it's understood
That there's beauty within you

But if we forget to show it
Then how are they to know
It's why we cannot love ourselves
It's what we need to show.

Untitled

There's too much space in this time
It leaves me restless, longing for
anything
Searching for a feeling to free me
Or give me an experience like in
the songs they sing.
I'm bottled up, closed off, and
drowned
By an emptiness and confusion that
lingers
Reaching to feel a touch, to burn
my skin
But it feels like liquid, cold – and
slips through my fingers
An explosion in my blood, a fire to
start
To excite me, thrill me – life that's
alive
But locked in this tiny room, still
imprisoned
Inside my head, my emotions once
again deprived.
Longing to love like never before,
just once
To feel that shock, that warmth,
slight of hand
To pull him near, without the pain
But fearing the truth, he'll
understand.
I want to be taken like the wind
And carried through life's tides,
and flown…
Through the stormy skies that
surround me
Into a place I've never known.
To be held close and not wanting
to move
From the quiet stillness, alive in
those arms
Able to dream away the nightmares

And be freed from the consuming
harm.
I wake to kiss him and hope for
truth
That when eyes have opened, he is
there
And when I tremble through the
nights
It's already understood, my past's
not fair.
For now in this moment, I've been
unbound
By that thread that held me deep
within
And I can shine in the sun's
beautiful day
And break the wall – the mask I
lived in.
For the reflection, the vision I hid
The mirror is true – a picture of me
Once I couldn't bare to look back
at
Now it's something better I see
In that mirror – it's a truer me.
And I love, for I waited for the
time
Stood patient and promised myself
a day
When I'd be let go by my trials and
pain
I could live with a passion and
forget yesterday.

Dream

Last night I had a dream
That left me trembling inside
It brought back a fear from long ago
One that I longed to leave behind.

I must be feeling more for you
For this to bring me so much pain
It was that feeling of such betrayal
That it would make me feel insane

When you trust and give so much of you
When you know you need someone
And then you fear they'll leave you
And you can't change what has begun

I felt so afraid last night, you see
It left me feeling all alone
So I know you must mean more to me
Because I feel how close to you I've grown

That I was scared you'd tire of me
Or that I wasn't good enough
I guess I want you to want me more
And having patience can be tough.

Untitled

Maybe I've just gotta be alone tonight
Not sure if I'll be all right
Hoping tomorrow will be a change
Right now my whole world feels strange

Feeling things I can't remember how
So long ago they disappeared…and now
All the emotions, all those fears
It all rushes back and I can't think clear

Is it ok, to want you more
It's not something I've needed before
My trust is at stake, if I give in
Afraid to tell you, what's held within

I know that I could love you
But question whether you feel it too
If I give too much, would you turn away
Would you understand, would you stay?

I want to hold on, but you might let go
What if I push too hard to let you know
So I spend my time and think my thoughts
Wondering if it's ok or if it's not.

Who's The One

Who's the one you think of
When your nights get long
Who makes your memories good ones
And who helps you right your wrongs

Who do you long to be with
All those nights when you're alone
Who's the one that makes you smile
When they call you on the phone

Do you ever feel they make life
A little brighter, every day
Do you long to spend a moment
Just to know her in a different way

Do you need her, do you want her
To feel the same as you
Have you ever asked her how she feels
And does she feel it too?

Because I ask myself the questions
And I spend time in my thoughts
And I often reach to touch you
But don't know if it's right or not.

Silent Friend

The words form then lay still upon my lips
And I keep silent – I cannot speak his name
I've remembered him in dreams when he has called to me
And in the restless nights, I know it's not the same
The frozen air brushes my skin and I tremble
And there is his face – softly lingering there
I know I cannot turn back, my hands frozen in time
The memory steals my breath and life proves to be unfair.
Youth burned out in a moment – the spark fades
And in the last light of innocence that soul dies
And takes with him so many unwept tears
Letting go of all the gray souls, all the pain and lies.
And my voice falls silent to the picture I hold of him
And I carry the ache of all the secrets I see in his eyes
The silent song that he longed to share with us
And that painful moment I feel, each time he cries.
So he lives within me as a true friend would
One whose life was given up too soon, one who left, alone
Leaving a memory of fiery hair and sun-burned smiles
In my doorway, the remembering is my own.
For such love in him was all we could see
Though every part of him screamed he was sad
Only in the morning's light did I ever know
We'd lost the truest man, purest friend we'd ever had.

Untitled

Sometimes I just step back and watch
And I see all the little things I miss each day
Because sometimes I rush through every minute
Thinking it'll change my life in some way
But it's those moments that slip by me
When I could have stopped to see why someone was crying
Instead of brushing them aside and going on
And later realizing I didn't understand because I wasn't trying
So today I held my breath and looked around
And noticed how a mother loved her baby
And how a friend laughed with another friend
And I paid attention to the life outside of me
And it's all part of me and of my world
And I make footprints on those things
Whether I ever realize it or not, it is my life
So if I take the time, imagine the life it would bring.

Words

I don't know what I'm trying to say
But I know how I feel here inside
I have trouble sometimes saying things
But it doesn't mean that I haven't tried

Right now my head says I'm a fool
And I should forget you, I don't know
Because my heart says something else
It tells me never let you go

This time around, I feel a distance
But I just can't read it in your eyes
Still, I've yet to spend the time with you
And I can't tell the truth from the lies.

And if you just don't want to see me
Could you tell me if this is true
Because I don't want to care, or try
If I'm only going to be hurt by you.

Untitled

I'm screaming inside
My heart's in pain
I heard them crying
And there was rain
An eerie silence
Across this land
The skies turned dark
The buildings to sand
A tear wells up
But is afraid to fall
I glimpse of hope
That our loved ones might call
A definite feeling
Consumes the air
Can't understand why
It just isn't fair
Now stand together
Stand brave, stand tall
Show all the world
There's justice for all.

Untitled

Trying to find some place inside
Away from the tragedies that weigh my heart
To seek an answer to set me free
Walk away, find an escape, find a start

My smile feels molded, it isn't me
I keep on searching for what is real
There is so much emptiness, no one knows
And such pain is all that I feel

Does any friend feel compassion here
Because it seems they only pretend to understand
Do they cry or do they hide their hearts
Are the promises simply erased, within the sand.

There's an endlessness to the never knowing
Wanting to be more than what they know of me
Feeling there is someone better hidden here
Someone I wish that they might see

But the will for strength, to stand up tall
Makes the weaker, emotional me pull back
Somehow what was all right as a child
Now shows weakness, something so many lack.

But late at night when alone, I think
And know that I could have a better life than this
If only I might set me free
I'd be living all the things I missed.

Untitled

Sometimes things are confusing
And that light I see by, it grows so dim
I feel sad when a man goes away
And I see the tears she cries for him

The world seems to be laughing
At all the things I sacrifice
But sometimes things must change
To make a life…turn out right

There are moments I can't remember
Others that just won't leave
Some special people who have come and gone
Some hurt me, and some made me believe

But I know someone, he's touched me
Some place I never allowed anyone to see
He gave me understanding and comfort
My soul and spirit finally felt free.

Lost

A hidden secret, so well kept
Unforgotten friend, she silently wept
Lost forever, be still this night
Fears to remember, alone in her fright
Longing to change what she knows she can't
Making a wish she knows God can't grant
A precious face, she still sees his smile
Nothing bad held, she thinks for a while
How deadly a drink, if only she'd known
If only he knew how much she has grown
Misunderstood, all those lonely tears
A hurt unseen, a mountain of fears
She watched him stumble, she saw the fall
So obvious, so oblivious, seen by all
Youth showed them nothing, how could it be
So much pain hidden where no one could see
If only she'd realized, this was her crime
She ran towards him, she's losing time
He broke the bottle, fell to the ground
Broken pieces of live, scattered around.

Untitled

When you dream of me, do you smile
And are you happy I am here
Do I make your days seem brighter
Do I make you see life more clear

When you think of me, are you worried
And is there confusion everywhere
Do I make you feel misunderstood
Is there distance in the air

When you tell me that you love me
Does it feel like it's a lie
Or do I mean so much to you
That you could not say goodbye

When you wake in the morning
Do you wish that I were there
And do I hurt you when I'm gone
Or do you know how much I care.

When you are lonely and restless
Do you long to feel my touch
Do I linger in your thoughts sometimes
Do I mean that much?

Untitled

Electric touch, I'm falling in
Burning flame, it's not a sin

His touch
Lightly, feeling like an electric shock
Causing her entire body to shake
And come to life.

The warmth
Of his lips pressed against hers
The wetness of his tongue
Finding hers, drawing her
Closer to him.

His strong
Yet gentle hands
Exploring her body, wanting her so much
Wanting it to be so perfect,
Trying to move slowly
Wanting to go
So fast.

Can't hide her need and desire
Her love for him burns like fire
Needing him, wanting him, more every night
He's her eternity, she knows it's right.

Untitled

Sometimes I feel so lost in time
I fall so hard and so fast
But the magic in the words you spoke
Made me believe, this time we'd last

Too naïve or just too hopeful
I don't know what it might be
Wanting your love to be stronger
Maybe that's why I was too blind to see

So now you've said it's over
And I can't believe you said goodbye
I still dream of you beside me
Until I wake alone and cry

I know you knew my feelings
So you must have known my pain
How long did you fight to say the words
That now you won't explain

So for now I carry a heavy weight
Of loss and love, I'll never share
The heart you held in your hands
Now says that love's not fair.

Untitled

There's not a moment I don't miss you
Though you may never make it here
Not a day passes that my love for you
Isn't overwhelming and crystal clear
I can't push ahead and make it spring
And hope for a miracle, that you will stay
Though my heart would always love you
I know the world doesn't work that way.
So if I could be a child and not realize
Then I think I'd pass my life on by
Waiting on a love that just won't come
No matter how hard I try
But I fear I'm older, and I know
Our love might never be
So I'll put you aside, a special man
Who holds a special place inside of me.
I'm not willing to forget you yet
The love I hold is so strong
I only wish it were different
For our timing was all wrong
I'll begin not to love you
A million years from now
If I could show you, you were worth it
But I simply don't know how
Maybe one day when you understand
Just how I love you so
Until you believe in the words I speak
Baby, I don't wanna know
Because you love someone else
And I can't break that apart
Forever and always I'll love you
And keep you safe within my heart.

Untitled

Heaviness sits around me this night
The chill so sharp and so dark
I feel paralyzed in fear, flashbacks
His face…my car…cold and piercing – a spark

I look over to the right – it's there, deserted
Almost the same as that night…that night
But it's a different town, a new place…same feeling
Inside I shake, I fear this, I don't want this fight

Why is the memory so clear, feels like it's happening again
But I'm older now, still burning with pain
I lock my doors, but it won't protect me from my head
Oh God, let this hurt wash away in the rain.

Short of breath, panicking, I can't think
It's an eerie silence between this night and me
It holds my secret; I hide this eternal fear
One night, like many still to be.

Untitled

Dark embrace my soul tonight
No slight of touch could make it right
Shady eyes search out that lie
A veil of deceit to hide my cry
One taste of bitter sweet and wrong
To hold forever what can't stay long
Surging fire through these veins
Consume the burn, before the rains
Silent eyes, mystery and a broken rose
The flame within her, no one knows.

Untitled

Forest fire…life beyond
So cold and out of touch
This life, to me, has lost its flame
And their looks don't move me much

Somewhere back in years gone by
My soul and heart collide
Bruised spirit from a painful time
What's true, her heart must hide

Together is not close enough
And love seemed to hurt too much
The look, the fire we held inside
And no passion in his touch.

Think

Do you think about your feelings
Are you confused by your thoughts
Do you think you've earned the life you have
Or did you pay for what you've got?

Did you always feel the heartache
And did life always seem unfair
When did you lose your smile
Was it when you thought that no one cared?

Does it ever really disappear
Or become something you can bare
Could someone help you learn to laugh
Or convince you they are there?

Is there some small bit of hope
Behind your beautiful, sullen eyes
Is there a glimpse of understanding
Knowing someone feels your cries?

Because in every labored breath you take
And every tear that's left behind
I feel these things inside of me
And I know what's in your mind.

Untitled

One day, one night
Please don't ask why
A smile, a laugh
Still alone she cries
Too soon, too late
And then she's gone
Too far, too close
Her dreams run on
So cold, so hot
Alone too long
So sweet, so pure
Her love so strong
Before, too soon
She carries the weight
A world, unknown
It can't be too late
To love, to give
Her life somewhere
To learn from loss
Someone will care.

Stranger

Disturbed by thoughts of black
And shadows of a faceless man
A fear that has taken hope of life
And his memory is her biggest fan.

Touch the heat that burns within her
The icy flesh begins to break
The strands of hair that strangle her
The innocence he forsakes

A tear so clear, so knowing
She knows he doesn't hear
The blood feels like a blanket
Like comfort from the fear

Uncaring, cold and naked
Her feelings and her life
His pungent breath, so wretched
And his blows just like a knife

Forever they are part of her
They cannot be erased
There is hope she'll find her special gift
That someone has misplaced.

Tragic

Before the darkness turned to light
Within the hours of that night
From laughter fall the tears of life
Reach in and steal them, turn the knife

From brightened eyes, a haze of gray
Swept up and bottled in that day
No turning back, changed for good
Changes in ways she never thought she would

Shadows watching all the time
Too friendly, too trusting, this was her crime
She can't escape her yesterdays
Life has changed her in so many ways

Cannot express all the piercing pain
Searching that thread of life to keep her same
Unbearable memories she locks away
Too fresh in her mind, always they stay

They remember a girl that she just can't be
She's hidden herself deep inside of me
Kept safe from a world that treated her cold
When she's scared or crying, she has me to hold.

Sleep

I can't remember peaceful sleep
Or nights of sweeter dreams
All the crumpled sheets I see
From fitful nights, it seems

One lost hour, one more smile
To hide the tired eyes
I mask the insomnia, my secret
As one more day slips slowly by

I hide the yawn, my weary soul
And I know that no one knows
The fears, the torment when I realize
That's just the way it goes

I don't know when the last night fell
And my eyes closed in sleep
To feel such calm and silence
When all those fears, God would keep.

Tonight, I don't even expect it
It's just like an old routine
But maybe this night will be different
Like a movie I haven't seen.

Life

It's not an easy life to live
The pain of every day
There's no open door to happiness
And I can't find my way

There are so many moments
When the fighting never ends
So many times my heart breaks
When his never even bends

The knots pull tighter deep inside
And the hurt crashes in on me
For a love that I might die for
A love he doesn't see

It doesn't take a genius
To know that I'm a fool
To love a man who says I love you
Just because he thinks it's cool

Still I pick up the pieces
And I'm still the one who stays
Though he seems to love another
And, from me, his heart strays

This life is not so easy
Even now, it twists and turns
My tears fall, in their knowing
Love is bitter, I have learned.

Reflecting

There are not many moments
When we can just be still
Look around us, at the world
And reflect on what we feel

There are so many angry people
And so many bitter fights
We turn away because it hurts
Too many silent nights

Searching for the answer
We need a reason why
Blaming love and turning cold
We learn to cheat and lie

But my darkness will pass
And my light will not fade
I'll look forward past this moment
And remember the choices that I made.

Untitled

A flash, a flood
Full of tears
Of pain.

Hurting to see
Him smile
When she is there

A twist inside
Tying me up
Binding me here

Love turns the page
Leaves me alone
Here

Trying to stay
Trying to disguise
My pain

As he smiles
Laughs ... and talks to
Her

Loving her
Saying it isn't
Real

But he is gone
He left long ago
For her

Untitled

I couldn't call it love
It was only hurtful and cheap
I never felt love there
Never felt a touch of kindness
Just an act to get me
Right where you needed me to be
To gain from what I had
And leave me feeling lost

But I didn't feel it either
And so my confusion just dragged on
Caught up in together
So I lost who I am
Became bitter, too tired and weak
To fight this out any more
So it had to end

Go your own way
And I will go mine
To lost souls together
Never made us whole

Restless

There is a quietness, a stillness in this night
Only a faint breath, the rest is blurred
No words spoken now, everyone is sleeping
In this night, that begs to be heard

Something seems to be missing here
Inside my head or maybe in my heart
I search for the dreams I thought I had
Growing restless for that new life to start

But still it remains empty and silent
Inside these walls I am held behind
Though invisible, I cannot break free
No place for the key to go…locked in my mind

I want to fight, I want to run
Leave all the painful memories scattered
But my feet are heavy and hold me here
Feeling my whole life is shattered

I know…I cannot let go
The silence, the remembering, the fear
I know…I cannot let go
Of the girl lost in that year.

Rage

A bitterness so cold and dark
Creeps inside of this hollow soul
An anger, a blame of everyone
Hopeless, playing the role

The irritable denial of something past
Something lost long ago
Draining the love from all I've held
And I didn't even know

Don't cry tears for me
For I have cried them all
I've been lost, the hurt has died
Still I cannot break the wall

Learning

Understand the pain
Of the tears I cry
Of feeling misunderstood
And never knowing why

Begin a search for something
Unknown what I will find
A quest for self acceptance
Leaves me feeling left behind

So a shiver and a chill
Settle deep within my soul
And the ones I push away
Are the ones who make me whole

So a broken promise
That I have now set free
A broken dream of a better life
You could live without me.

Their Voices

The voices came upon her
she could hear her mother well
she wanted to reach out to her
but on her, the curtain fell

So she couldn't cry in sorrow
and she couldn't reach her hand
she wanted to give something
to help her mother understand

Her mind slept in darkness
empty thoughts rolled through her mind
she couldn't find a shred of light
all life wasleft behind.

four days had passed around her
when she opened up her eyes
when she looked she found a lifetime
as she heard her family's cries

And she never had a doubt again
about where she should be
she found so much to live for
there was so much life left to see.

Online

It's her again, online
It sounds so stupid
So insane
It's her again
Who made him smile
When he asked if he
Could talk to her
It's her
Who he wants to call
Her
Who hears 'I love you'
It's her again
Under some new name
Trying to hide from
Me
This internet thing
Can hurt as bad
As real life
Sometimes.
Does he really
Love her?
Or is it a lie?
And if it is
Does he love me?
Or is it a lie?
What plans are made
Where might they meet?
Why does he care so much
And what about me?
I can't take it
Finding her number
Knowing he calls her
And tells her
He loves her forever.
What about me, What about me
Have I lost him…to her again?

Angie
(Jagger/Richards)

Oh, Angie, Oh, Angie, when will those dark clouds disappear
Angie, Angie, where will it lead us from here
With no loving in our souls and no money in our coats
You can't say we're satisfied

But Angie, Angie, you can't say we never tried
Angie, you're beautiful, but ain't it time we said goodbye

Angie, I still love you, remember all those nights we cried
All the dreams we held so close seemed to all go up in smoke
Let me whisper in your ear
Angie, Angie, where will it lead us from here

Oh, Angie, don't you weep, all your kisses still taste sweet
I hate that sadness in your eyes
But Angie, Angie, ain't it time we said goodbye
With no loving in our souls and no money in our coats
You can't say we're satisfied
But angie, I still love you baby, ev'rywhere I look I see your eyes
There ain't a woman that comes close to you, come on baby, dry your eyes
But Angie, Angie ain't it good to be alive
Angie, Angie, they can't say we never tried

Time

Another year has come and passed
Funny how the years don't last
And yet I sit here and reminisce
Knowing there are memories I will miss

This time of year I often cry
I can't explain it, I don't know why
Maybe because my family means so much
And I keep you safe someplace that no bad could touch

And as the nights get chilly and my feet get cold
I realize we all fit perfectly into life's mold
And I see so much beauty in each one of you
So much difference, and yet likeness in all that we do

Yet still we're the same, our family is one
Though one is the moon, the other the sun
Through all of life's changing, the bond is strong
We comfort each other, when something goes wrong

And the love remains unconditioned, gentle and pure
For all of our weaknesses, it's family that cures
And I feel through the miles, through the mountains between
Only you understand completely the trials we've seen

The bridge that connects us in our hearts and souls
It drives us all as we reach for our goals
And so with this said, though I cannot be there
There's no other on earth, with whom I could share

Such love of family, such hope for life
I'll be with you always, through joys and through strife
And I'm praying and wishing, this holiday
That my love will surround you, along the way.

Untitled

It seems like so long ago, when I first saw true beauty
it seems so distant when I think back and realize what it means to care
And every day there is something new to find hope in
still so many lives I can touch, and dreams just waiting for someone to
share.
It feels like a million years have passed since I first smiled
and took the hand of someone that I truly trusted with my heart
And yet it was only yesterday that I remembered how to trust
and it was only yesterday I thought about how my life would start
Because sometimes I take for granted that I breathe, that I laugh
and I forget that a kind word changes lives in ways I never understood
Yesterday I wished for more money and an easier life for myself
and never stopped for a moment to think that I ever would
Today I dreamed of Christmas and of New Year's and of family
and I found myself at peace, and I realized my dream
That it isn't money or material that makes me happy and good
that the small things make life more then what it seems
So I can be who I am without worry of what they will think
and I can help another and be proud of that, even if it's simple and small
And I can write a note or a poem to express my feelings for someone
so long as I express them, because without that no one could know me at
all
And I believe in you, and I believe in a life that's full
of all the things that I myself put into it through the years
And I know that my simple poem and my spoken words
will reach you in laughter, smiles, sorrows and in tears

So perhaps the only thing I really need then is to speak to you
through my heart, and within my soul...touching a place where you'll
forever hold me
And that is all I need...you...part of me in love and honesty
because inside of me, this is the safest place that you could ever be.

I See

The haze inside your head
Doesn't hide your tears from me
Like a gentle rain in your eyes
Sad, still softly it sets me free

The time that spins out of control
You hesitate to look within
An unconditional understanding
Of a love I cannot win

A season filled of spreading joy
Holds a silent loneliness for some
A longing to hold you close forever
Though the time might never come

A special heart for caring
To be held by your warmth for a while
A prayer for just the chance to be
The reason for your smile

I could give my love to you each day
And give it twice on Sunday
For you hold my trust inside your hand
And you could hold my heart today

I believe in you maybe more
Than even you could see
And your friendship is always special
Because you believe in me.

12-08-01

He Never Even Knew Me

He never even knew me;
I was just in the wrong place
I thought he needed help from
me,
and he had such a sweet face.
He just seemed so nervous,
always on the edge of his seat.
I couldn't see through the
darkness,
and I began to get cold feet.
He really seemed quite stupid,
and soon he had me lost.
I thought, "I'd like to call a cab
for him
no matter what the cost."
The streets were dark and quiet,
and I had no clue where we were.
I felt the knots inside my
stomach,
and my intuitions stir.
But I tossed aside the worries
and thought, "It's just silly me."
This poor guy needed someone's
help;
this is where God wants me to
be.
We stopped at a convenience
store
so he could use the phone.
I thought he should call his sister
because we couldn't find her
home.
I looked around the parking lot,
and God, I so wanted to go.
I had so many choices then,
but I just didn't know.
I saw him, he was coming back,

and I just held my breath.
He said, "She's only a mile
away."
Thank God there's just one mile
left.
Back on the street, so dark and
cold.
Man, I didn't like this street.
There was a sign, what did it
say?
I felt so tired and so beat.
I was confused, it couldn't be,
did the sign say what I thought it
said?
I asked him, "Did that sign say
'Dead End'?"
Was that what I had read?
Inside I felt so sick and scared,
as I tried to turn around.
I hoped I could get out of this,
still there was no light to be
found.
He kept telling me to watch it
or we might end up in the ditch.
I wished he'd sit back and just
shut up,
because all he did was bitch.
I finally had the car turned
around
so I could go back to the store.
Let his sister come and pick him
up,
because I could take no more.
And that's when it happened,
as I tried to get my car to go.
He slipped it into neutral,
and I didn't even know.

Such fear rose from inside of me,
but I tried not to let it show.
But when I saw into his eyes,
the fear began to grow.
I tried to drive away again,
when his hand grabbed my wrist.
"Oh God, no! Is this happening?"
I saw him make a fist.
His eyes looked crazy through
the dark,
the only thing that I could see.
Through a night filled with
blackness,
was this happening to me?
A blur of pain and darkness,
a fear so deep and strong
A haze of blood and silent cries,
in a night, my life went wrong.
The golden thread of life, which
held me,
and bound me to a world, so cold
Broken when he beat and raped
me,
and the tragedy unfolds.
My breath slowed, and my body
just went limp, I lost control.
I didn't cry. God, was I dying?
I can't describe all that he stole.
He threw me on the frozen
ground,
and he kicked at me some more.
I guess he figured what the hell,
what else is she good for?
When he thought he took my life
from me,
and I was close enough to death
I heard him as he rushed away,
and still I held my breath.
When the car had been started,
still on the ground I laid.

The grass my warmth and
blanket,
so there is where I stayed.
When those two taillights had
faded,
I slowly lifted up my head.
The fear inside left me shaking.
'God, could I be dead?'
I didn't know if he'd be back,
so I got up and tried to run
I had to find a place that's safe
from what this man had done.
He never even knew me;
I was just in the wrong place.
He made me feel sick inside;
I couldn't look him in the face.
It's not the end of the story,
oh no, there's so much more
I found a house to go to,
but they wouldn't open up their
door.
Please, someone help me,
please don't let this man come
back.
I promise not to scare you,
but I know he will be back.
The next house opened up their
door
and quickly pulled me inside
Covered up my naked body,
which I quickly tried to hide.
I made it through the terror,
but my fear is always there
I could never forget the feelings
or the pain that I must bare.
I know my life's worth living,
but sometimes when I'm alone
I realize some things I go
through;
I must go through on my own.

And no one knows my losses
because they are simply mine
Other survivors understand me,
and our stories, somehow are
intertwined.

He never even knew me;
I was just in the wrong place.
My intuitions told me,
now I will never forget his face.

Losing Control

The softest touch and there is a fire
so overwhelmed with this desire
his burning fingers, the sweat of skin
pulls me near him, beautiful sin

I touch his shoulder, he touches my hair
if the world fell apart I wouldn't care
aching inside to be all he needs
my heart surrenders, slowly it bleeds

my lips search him, draw him near
breathing his breath, my actions are clear
tasting the salt from the sweat of his skin
knowing my passion will soon let him in

tender and biting, bodies set free
knowing I want him, does he want me?
my body is burning, electric air
hold on to a moment, if you dare

urging him forward, I'm in control
longing to have him, he'll make me whole
my tongue needing more of him, deeper inside
come to the place where I cannot hide

touch me, come over me like a wave
never thought I could ever give what I gave
bodies together, wet and sweet
be inside me, here we will meet

a surge of pain, a single tear
explosion of passion, a moment of fear
legs wrapped together, his love in me
I lost control, I'm finally free.

I could speak endlessly about writing and how it is my passion and my love in life, but I don't think it could ever truly express how writing makes me feel. Writing is therapy for me, it is a friend to me and it is a release for me. I don't sit here each day and think relentlessly about what I want to write or what feelings I just have to express to someone, it just isn't like that.

I am just writing. I write when my mind is flooded with emotions that are just rushing and pouring through me like a waterfall. It's like a magic I could never hope to share in the way it should be. Writing takes me to the warmest beaches and the highest mountains. It takes me through heaven and into paradise. Sometimes it pushes me into my greatest fears and most deadly situations. Through all the journeys, though, writing has left me, in the end, at peace. It has left me at peace with the world and myself. It has opened me up and made me look inside myself and get to know who I am.

Writing has given me a voice that I never knew I had. Silent for so long, I finally found a way to give and share a part of myself that I have longed for someone to notice in me. Writing has no definition, no limits, no rules. Whether it is a rhyme, or a story, or a verse, or a quote, it is a feeling like breathing in the sweet air of summer, or a breeze that lightly caresses your face.

I write because it feels good. Writing makes everything inside of me come to life. It pulls from deep inside of me, and explodes onto the paper. It's like a silent scream that has been suppressed for so long, and when you finally let go of it, you feel fresh and clean. Writing is my way to cry about all the painful memories that ever happened in my life, which I just couldn't cry about before. This is how I feel when I write.

There are places within all of us that are untouched by the trials in life. There are those spaces between heartache and love that you may never see, but they are there. They are the places that, if we're lucky, we will realize are the greatest places to have. Where we realize that love has pain, and without pain we would not be the people we are. I think about this every day, as I go through my life feeling lonely or lost, or being so in love with someone who seldom returns that love. I know that I long for the pain sometimes just to know I am still alive. I think that I sometimes take for granted that I have the ability to feel pain, as well as to feel sadness, to feel happiness, and to feel love for someone other than myself. That is what is so great about life and about being human. We are allowed to feel and to learn and to express this to others in remarkable ways.

I know that my heart aches every single time I think of my baby sister. Every time I long to just kiss her or hold her. I cry when I think that she is so perfect and so beautiful and so innocent. When I wish I could have a baby of my own someday and wonder if that is even possible. I ache when I think how lucky Mom is to have such a beautiful thing as Tori…and how she is so deserving of that.

And in the end, I appreciate that I can feel this and that I know inside that those feelings make me good and they make me less selfish. They tell me that I am capable of loving in a way that some may never know. Because I can cry openly and feel things so strongly, and take things so personally. Because I am me and that is a wonderful thing.

I am twenty-four years old and I have been places and seen things that many never have and hopefully some things that others never will . I have been in that deep, dark hole and there were moments when I thought it was the end. I have been to the bottom of the bottom, and when I thought all was lost, something or someone was there, reaching out to me, comforting me and lending a hand. And so now even when I am feeling lonely and as if no one loves me, I know in my heart that isn't true, because even though I don't have a love of my own…I have the love of my family and my friends. And no matter what, that is the greatest gift I could ever have.

I don't know why I am writing all this here. Maybe it is because I know that I am not the only person who has these feelings, and yet I wonder if the others who feel this way realize that there is someone who cares. I guess I want to share that with the rest of you out there. If you really have no one then you can have me. I will be your friend if you need one, I will be the one who listens when you need someone to hear. I feel like it is the only contribution I can make that might really help someone else get through the hard times. Until you feel good again, and know how wonderful you must be. Until you can look in a mirror and be ok with the image that you see. Until you know that no person is perfect and being who you are is all you can be. There is a spirit locked up in there that longs to scream out and here is where I hope you can do that. If you need a friend...I will be there. Maybe in the shadows but always close by. I know what it's like to need a friend, just someone who will listen and understand I don't know why I am writing all this here. Maybe it is because I know that I am not the only person who has these feelings, and yet I wonder if the others who feel this way realize that there is someone who cares. I guess I want to share that with the rest of you out there. If you really have no one then you can have me. I will be your friend if you need one, I will be the one who listens when you need someone to hear. I feel like it is the only contribution I can make that might really help someone else get through the hard times. Until you feel good again, and know how wonderful you must be. Until you can look in a mirror and be ok with the image that you see. Until you know that no person is perfect and being who you are is all you can be. There is a spirit locked up in there that longs to scream out and here is where I hope you can do that. If you need a friend...I will be there. Maybe in the shadows but always close by. I know what it's like to need a friend, just someone who will listen and understand without judgment.

Everyone who has opened this book has become my friend...taken the journey with me through all the years of writing. I hope to hear from you all...share your stories, your poetry, your pain and tears. Share your inspirations or memories with me.

Peace and Love to you all...

Angie

ABOUT THE AUTHOR

I am 44 years old. I currently live in Owasso, Oklahoma. I spent 11 years, from 1998 – 2009, in Las Vegas, Nevada. Poetry was my first love ... I started writing about 7 years old.

I think I have written these poems to my Kendall, Amelia, and Dawson ... they are my nieces and nephew, and they truly are the most special. Poetry should speak to each reader differently and personally, so while the poems reflect moments in my life, hopefully they help you find the words to express moments in your own life.

Made in the USA
Coppell, TX
03 May 2024

31989587R00094